A Mom's Book of Adventure

THIS BOOK BELONGS TO

....

 Find us on Facebook and join the community of moms!
facebook.com/WhereMomsConnect

Loveland, Colorado | group.com

Group resources really work!

This Group resource incorporates our R.E.A.L. approach to ministry. It reinforces a growing friendship with Jesus, encourages long-term learning, and results in life transformation, because it's:

Relational—Learner-to-learner interaction enhances learning and builds Christian friendships.

Experiential—What learners experience through discussion and action sticks with them up to 9 times longer than what they simply hear or read.

Applicable—The aim of Christian education is to equip learners to be both hearers and doers of God's Word.

Learner-based—Learners understand and retain more when the learning process takes into consideration how they learn best.

A Mom's Book of Adventure

Visit our website: **group.com/women**

This resource is brought to you by the wildly creative women's ministry team at Group. Additional moms who contributed to this book include:

Linda Crawford
Jan Kershner
Susan Lawrence
Cheryl Meakins
Jill Wuellner

Unless otherwise indicated, all Scripture quotations are taken from the *Holy Bible*, New Living Translation, copyright © 1996, 2004, 2007 by Tyndale House Foundation. Used by permission of Tyndale House Publishers, Inc., Carol Stream, Illinois 60188. All rights reserved.

ISBN 978-1-4707-1321-8

Printed in the United States of America.

10 9 8 7 6 5 4 3 2 1   23 22 21 20 19 18 17 16 15 14

····Contents····

Welcome
to
....A Year of....
ADVENTURE

There's no doubt about it—being a mom is an adventure. You may not ever go skydiving, white-water rafting, or bungee jumping, but from the moment you hear you're expecting your first child, a different kind of adventure begins. One that is at times thrilling, terrifying, exciting, and even risky.

This year as you join with other moms at Where Moms Connect, you'll explore different aspects of the adventure of motherhood, and through it all, you'll also find encouragement to lift your heart and encouragement in your relationship with God.

This book will be your guide every step of the way. Tucked in these pages are all the notes, Bible verses, reflections, and other content you'll need to participate each time you gather at Where Moms Connect. Be sure to bring this book along when you meet.

We know that as a mom you're busy. But we also know you care about growing yourself spiritually, emotionally, and mentally. So along with the content for each session of Where Moms Connect, we've included additional notes for you to read and reflect on if you have time. Sometimes it's a devotion, sometimes a few verses, other times just a short thought to reflect on. These are for you to use as you want, as you have time, with no guilt and no pressure.

Thanks for joining other moms at Where Moms Connect. We hope this truly is a year of adventure for you on your journey in momhood.

Kickoff to *Adventure*

Connecting to the Topic

- How would you define the word "adventure"?

_____

_____

_____

_____

_____

_____

_____

Surviving the Adventure

Directions

1. Individually read the information describing the situation.

2. Rank the items in the first list alone, without asking for help from your group.

3. Once you and the others in your group have completed the first part alone, join together and use the second list to reach a consensus on the best ranking for each item.

The Situation

Your group has become lost in Minnesota in a wilderness area made up of thick woods near many lakes and streams. Nobody knows you are there. The snow depth ranges from just above the ankles to knee deep. The temperature is 25 degrees in the daytime and -40 degrees at night. There is plenty of dead wood and twigs in the immediate area. You are dressed in clothing appropriate for city wear—suits, pants, street shoes, and overcoats.

Your group has eight items. You need to rank these items according to their importance to your survival, starting with 1 for the most important and ending with 8 for the least important.

Complete this ranking on your own.

__ball of steel wool   __hand ax

__family-size chocolate bar   __can of shortening
  (1 per person)

                        __cigarette lighter

__compass   (without fluid)

__extra shirt and pants for   __a quart of 100-proof whiskey
  each survivor

Now join with the members of your group and discuss your rankings for each item. Then decide, as a group, on one consensus ranking for the importance of each item.

Complete this ranking as a group.

__ball of steel wool   __hand ax

__family-size chocolate bar   __can of shortening
  (1 per person)

                        __cigarette lighter

__compass   (without fluid)

__extra shirt and pants for   __a quart of 100-proof whiskey
  each survivor

Two—or More—Are Better Than One

Reflection Questions

Take a few minutes to discuss these questions with another mom in your group.

• You had to figure out the best decision to make in the survival adventure you just experienced. How was this experience similar to what you experience in parenting? How was it different?

_____

_____

_____

• When you have to make parenting decisions, when do you seek advice from other moms? What causes you to determine that you need insights from someone else?

_____

_____

_____

Connecting With God

• Why would a group have a better chance of survival than an individual?

_____

_____

_____

In your group, one mom can read this Bible verse aloud. Then discuss the question below.

Two in a bed warm each other. Alone, you shiver all night. By yourself you're unprotected. With a friend you can face the worst. Can you round up a third? A three-stranded rope isn't easily snapped. (Ecclesiastes 4:11-16, The Message)

Discuss:

- How can being a part of Where Moms Connect help you experience the benefits listed in this verse?

_____

_____

_____

Another mom in the group can read this Bible verse; then discuss the following questions with your group.

Just think—you don't need a thing, you've got it all! All God's gifts are right in front of you as you wait expectantly for our Master Jesus to arrive on the scene for the Finale. And not only that, but God himself is right alongside to keep you steady and on track until things are all wrapped up by Jesus. God, who got you started in this spiritual adventure, shares with us the life of his Son and our Master Jesus. He will never give up on you. Never forget that. (1 Corinthians 1:7-9, The Message)

Discuss:

- What promises from God can you see in this passage of Scripture?

_____

_____

_____

- How can these promises become your "survival" gear for your adventures of motherhood?

_____

_____

_____

Connecting to My Life

- Something I've discovered today that I want to remember and apply:

_____

_____

_____

_____

_____

_____

Additional Thoughts on Heading Into Adventure

An adventure is only an inconvenience rightly considered. An inconvenience is only an adventure wrongly considered. —Gilbert K. Chesterton

- What "inconveniences" in your life could you begin to consider as adventures instead?

_____

_____

_____

_____

_____

- How could this change of perspective on those "inconveniences" help you enjoy the adventures of motherhood more?

_____

_____

_____

_____

_____

_____

_____

_____

_____

_____

_____

_____

_____

_____

_____

_____

_____

_____

Don't run from tests and hardships, brothers and sisters. As difficult as they are, you will ultimately find joy in them; if you embrace them, your faith will blossom under pressure and teach you true patience as you endure. And true patience brought on by endurance will equip you to complete the long journey and cross the finish line—mature, complete, and wanting nothing. (James 1:2-4, The Voice)

- Using this Scripture as a guide, write a prayer to God for the patience and endurance you need and for the joy you want to find in the challenging journey of motherhood.

_____

_____

_____

_____

_____

_____

_____

_____

_____

_____

_____

_____

_____

Notes

_____

_____

_____

_____

_____

_____

_____

_____

_____

_____

_____

_____

_____

_____

_____

_____

_____

When *Life* Is a *Circus*

Connecting to the Topic

Lessons From the Big Top

- Push yourself; see how far you can go.

- Open new doors; explore new things.

- Reach out to others; help them succeed.

- Accept help and coaching from others.

- Be part of something bigger than yourself.

Connecting With God

As Jesus was walking along, he saw a man named Matthew sitting at his tax collector's booth. "Follow me and be my disciple," Jesus said to him. So Matthew got up and followed him. (Matthew 9:9)

Connecting to My Life

- Tell about a time you felt God nudging you to do something. What did you do, and how did it turn out?

_____

_____

Additional Thoughts on Dealing With Life When It Feels Like a Circus

"I came that they may have life and have it abundantly."
—Jesus (John 10:10, New American Standard)

With this in mind, choose one of the ideas below to experience living life more abundantly this week.

• Think about a particular challenge you are facing in your life right now. What life lessons have you learned or are you learning because of it?

• With your family, take an evening to play a game together or watch a movie that will enable you to laugh and just enjoy being together.

• Think of something in your life that you've put off doing because it scares you—maybe a conversation you need to have with someone close to you or taking that class you've always wanted to take. Take the beginning steps toward doing that thing.

• Take time with your family to do something you've never done before—maybe serving meals at a homeless shelter or running a race together.

• Think of a woman you would like to get to know better, and invite her out for coffee and a time of conversation.

• Think of something you've attempted in the past but been unsuccessful at, and try it again.

• As a family, get involved in some sort of serving opportunity—maybe meeting the need of a family in your church or neighborhood or collecting money for a charitable organization.

• Think of an area in your life where you're not feeling very successful—maybe as a mom or in your spiritual life. Find another woman you think could help you move forward in that area, and ask her to get together with you to talk about it.

Guilt-Free Mom Time

Connecting Together

Just for Me

- What would you love to do just for yourself? And what ideas did you get from others in your group?

_____

_____

_____

Connecting to the Topic

Discuss:

- Do you think Cloud and Townsend are right that moms tend to be more "we" oriented than "me" oriented? Explain your reasons for your answer.

_____

_____

_____

- When have you felt guilty about doing something just for you?

_____

_____

_____

- What are reasons moms might feel guilty about caring for their own needs?

_____

_____

_____

- What might be negative results of a mom neglecting her own needs? What might happen?

_____

_____

_____

Connecting With God

One woman can read this paragraph aloud to the table group:

In Luke 5:12-16, we see what it looks like to take care of our own needs while also taking care of the needs of others. This section of the Bible tells how Jesus heals a man with leprosy. After Jesus healed the man, "vast crowds came to hear him preach and to be healed of their diseases. But Jesus often withdrew to the wilderness for prayer."

Discuss:

- We may not have actual vast crowds clamoring for us to help them and heal them, but we may sometimes feel like this! For Jesus, the wilderness was a place where he could get away from people and responsibilities for a time. When you need to get away from people and responsibilities, where could you go?

_____

_____

_____

- When Jesus withdrew to the wilderness, the way he took care of himself was to pray. When you withdraw to your wilderness, what do you do to care for yourself?

_____

_____

_____

- What's your greatest barrier to caring for yourself in this way?

_____

_____

_____

Connecting to My Life

In the chart below, write a few of your own ideas for ways you can take care of yourself; then share your ideas with others in your group. As you hear ideas from others that you like, add them to your own chart.

Daily

_____

_____

_____

_____

Monthly

_____

_____

_____

_____

Yearly

_____

_____

_____

_____

Additional Thoughts on Guilt-Free Mom Time

The Lord is my shepherd; I have all that I need. He lets me rest in green meadows; he leads me beside peaceful streams. He renews my strength. (Psalm 23:1-3)

Take a moment and think about a recent experience you had when you felt the need for peace. Perhaps it was today in the slow checkout line at your local superstore. Or last week stuck in traffic and late for an appointment.

In our busy lives, a moment of peace would be a special treat—like the little chocolate left on our pillow at a luxury hotel. Have you ever eaten that chocolate and felt guilty later? If we took the time for a "peace treat"—a moment of rest in our strenuous schedule—would we feel guilty too?

When was the last time you enjoyed a "peace treat"? We women commonly experience more stress than peace in our lives. This is a real problem for us. Medical research estimates as much as 90 percent of our illnesses and diseases are stress-related. And, as women, we are nearly twice as likely as men to be afflicted with them.

Stress is making us sick! We need peace as a daily requirement for health! Let's get practical. We need to get an everyday dose of "peace treats," like a hot cup of tea, a nap, or a good book. But, unfortunately, without Jesus even these will be incomplete.

The good news is that Jesus has given us a free gift of peace, and it's available anytime and anywhere! The Bible says this peace is different from the peace the world can give us. That peace can give us rest, but God gives us peace of mind and heart!

We need more peace—both as the world gives and as Jesus gives. We need to give to ourselves those "peace treats" of the restful activities we enjoy, and we need to ask for the wonderful "gift of peace" only Jesus can give.

How do you receive his peace? Add some Scripture meditation or prayer to your tea time. Ask Jesus for peace of mind the next time you're in the slow checkout line or stressing out over life. He's got peace, and he can give it! Indulge yourself—enjoy some "peace treats" with Jesus and forget the guilt!

Notes

_____

_____

_____

_____

_____

_____

_____

_____

_____

_____

_____

_____

_____

_____

_____

_____

What's Right With You:
The surprising truth about self-worth

Connecting to the Topic

I Am...

HELLO! I am...

Restoration

• Ideas for helping me boost my sense of self-worth are...

_____

_____

_____

_____

_____

Expert Opinions

- Filter.

- Quit comparing.

- Do something you're good at.

Connecting to My Life

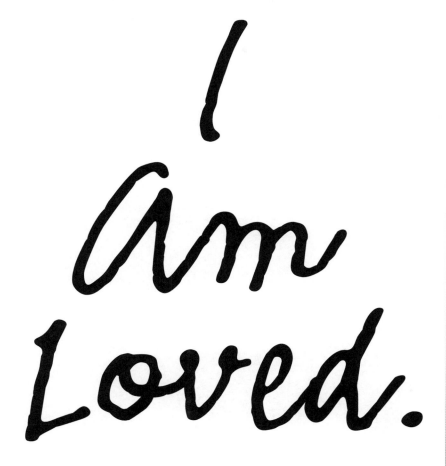

"For we are God's masterpiece. He has created us anew in Christ Jesus, so we can do the good things he planned for us long ago."

(Ephesians 2:10)

Additional Thoughts About Self-Worth

It's easy to let negative thoughts about ourselves crowd our minds. Take a few minutes to read this devotion and consider how you might give someone else a much-needed boost of positivity.

Think of ways to encourage one another to outbursts of love and good deeds. (Hebrews 10:24)

Sadly, I tossed it in the trash. According to the tag, my gorgeous orchid plant required just three ice cubes a week... seemed simple enough. I'm a bit embarrassed to say that before long, the last petal of the gorgeous, amethyst-colored flower dried up and fell off. Busyness kept my mind away from this simple three-ice-cube task.

No big deal, right? I still subconsciously must have recognized this dead plant as failure, for the thought crept into my mind, "I am no good at this!" I snickered to myself—it is just a plant, I know. Yet these three ice cubes seemed to raise up three words inside my head. And with these three words came feelings that echoed inside me as I dropped the dead plant in the garbage... *inadequate, incapable,* and *incompetent.* As I threw the plant away, I realized I had also thrown away my confidence.

Do you ever feel "no good at this"?

A sweet, encouraging girlfriend gave me the orchid plant; but as I threw it away, I ironically thought of the people in my life that criticized more than encouraged.

God intends for us to live with confidence and encourage one another. I know this and felt that the Lord was bringing me back to the three words that echoed in my head: *inadequate, incapable, incompetent.* Then I remembered times when God nudged me to jump *in,* speak *in,* or step *in* and help another. I'm about as good at this as I am at watering my plants sometimes.

We can lovingly step *in* and help another by simple words of encouragement—words that change *in*adequate to *adequate*, *in*capable to *capable*, and *in*competent to *competent*.

As I came in from throwing away the orchid plant, I passed by my flower garden outside, which just happens to need more than three ice cubes a week; thankfully, it's on its own watering system. Like you and me and our circle of girlfriends, there were some thriving flowers and some wilting flowers. Like the flowers, some of us are flourishing and thriving—maybe someone remembered their three-ice cubes…ha-ha!

Like flowers, we grow with helpful soil, and we help one another "burst" from the soil by watering with our words of encouragement. You never know when your words will pour into the recesses of another's mind to help and keep them from throwing away their confidence. They may just need three ice cubes a week.

Is there someone in your life who appears to be wilting from lack of encouragement? Take the time to write her a note with three things you appreciate about her as a way of watering her soul.

_____

_____

_____

_____

_____

_____

_____

_____

Childhood Development:

How children (and their parents) grow

Connecting to the Topic

Exploring Social and Emotional Development

Activity 1: When children are 6 months to 4 years

The mom in your pair who has the shortest hair will go first. Explain what you had for breakfast this morning, using only your hands—no words. The other mom will use words to guess what you are trying to say. Try to get your partner to name the specifics of your breakfast. For example, get her to say "juice" or "coffee" rather than "drink." After about a minute, switch so the other mom communicates with only her hands.

From ages 6 months to 3 or 4 years old, children are acquiring language skills.

Discuss:

• What emotions did you feel as you were trying to communicate without the use of words?

_____

_____

• As you were guessing what the other mom was "saying," how did you help her communicate with you better?

_____

_____

- How does this help you remember what it's like for a child in the middle of acquiring language skills?

_____

_____

Activity 2: When children are 4 to 9 years

Each person in your pair should draw a tiger in the space below. Take only 1 minute to complete your drawing, but in that time, draw the most beautiful and active and amazing tiger you can imagine. After you are both finished drawing, show your picture to your partner.

Discuss:

- What were your personal expectations for your own drawing? What did you *want* to show or imagine in your mind?

_____

_____

- How does this relate to what you actually were *able* to draw?

_____

_____

From ages 4 to 9 a child is able to identify general emotions such as being happy or mad (just as you were likely able to draw the general outline of a tiger). However, they are not always able to name more specific emotions such as frustration, disappointment, or embarrassment (just as you were likely not able to include great detail and skill in your drawing). They may not be sure why they feel those emotions or what to do with them.

Allowing our children to grow into their understanding of their emotional responses is the starting point for helping them make healthy decisions in their relationships.

Discuss:

• How might this activity help you understand your child's experience in relating to others?

_____

_____

Activity 3: When children are 8 to 18 years

The person wearing the most blue should draw a picture in the space below of either a cowboy or a princess. Take 1 minute to draw. The other mom will call out a new suggestion or idea on what the drawing should look like at least once every 10 seconds. The mom who is calling out ideas will say "stop" when a minute is up. Then switch roles.

Discuss:

- How did you feel when you were trying to incorporate the suggestions from your partner?

_____

_____

- How do you think children who are in the "tween and teen" years feel about trying to incorporate suggestions you make?

_____

_____

At this stage of life, kids are in the process of finding their own adventure called life! This is a slow transition as parents move from having control over every decision to guiding kids in making their own choices. It's the launch pad for teaching your kids independent self-assessment and about making wise choices.

Discuss:

- What changes might you need to make to move from _directing_ your tween/teenager to _guiding_ him or her?

_____

_____

Connecting With God

Read the Scripture verses and discuss the questions below.

Like newborn babies, you must crave pure spiritual milk so that you will grow into a full experience of salvation. Cry out for this nourishment, now that you have had a taste of the Lord's kindness. (1 Peter 2:2-3)

- How is our spiritual growth like or unlike the physical growth of a child?

_____

_____

- What do you think "spiritual milk" is?

_____

_____

- What encouragement can you take from this passage?

_____

_____

My child, pay attention to what I say. Listen carefully to my words. Don't lose sight of them. Let them penetrate deep into your heart, for they bring life to those who find them, and healing to their whole body. (Proverbs 4:20-22)

- Imagine these words are spoken by God the Father to you as his child. What do they say to you about God's heart toward you and your growth?

_____

_____

_____

- Reading the Bible is one way we can hear God's word. What are other ways you can pay attention to and think about what God is saying to you?

_____

_____

_____

Connecting to My Life

Reflect on the following questions, and write down any ideas that come to mind.

- What new strategy of parenting might you implement this week?

_____

_____

_____

_____

- In what ways do you believe God is nurturing your growth right now?

_____

_____

_____

_____

Additional Thoughts on Child Development

The Bible uses many metaphors to communicate how God helps us grow. Read Colossians 2:7 this week, and use the following suggestions to reflect on your own growth.

Let your roots grow down into him, and let your lives be built on him. Then your faith will grow strong in the truth you were taught, and you will overflow with thankfulness. (Colossians 2:7)

- Ask God to show you ways your roots can grow deeper into him.

_____

_____

_____

_____

_____

_____

_____

_____

- What are ways that being rooted in God has caused your faith to flourish? Use the space below to write a short note of overflowing thankfulness to God.

_____

_____

_____

_____

_____

_____

_____

_____

_____

_____

_____

_____

_____

_____

_____

_____

_____

_____

_____

_____

_____

The *Mystery* of *Autism*

Connecting to the Topic

Locate the indicator of autism that corresponds with your assigned number, read the description, and follow the instructions exactly during the small-group activity.

Indicator #1: Mental Limitations

Your most prominent indicator of autism is a mental limitation. You can only discuss a narrow range of topics, and your current favorite is "race cars."

Throughout the small-group conversation, *talk about race cars and only race cars.*

Indicator #2: Physical Barriers and Social Restrictions

Your most prominent indicators of autism are a physical barrier and a social restriction. You don't make eye contact with anyone—*ever.*

Throughout the small-group conversation, *constantly look down and rock back and forth as you participate.*

Indicator #3: Altered Communication Skills

Your most prominent indicator of autism has to do with your altered communication skills. You never use the words "me" or "I."

Throughout the small-group conversation, if you talk about yourself, *always refer to yourself by your first name.*

Indicator #4: Compulsive Behavior

Your most prominent indicator of autism has to do with compulsive behavior. You're obsessed with a pen on your table.

Throughout the small-group conversation, *focus all your energy, movement, and communication around the pen.*

Connecting With God

Don't be afraid, for I am with you. Don't be discouraged, for I am your God. I will strengthen you and help you. (Isaiah 41:10)

A message from Patch

My name is Patrick Anderson (otherwise known as the person in the video on autism). You may also call me Patch. The reason I used the word disease to describe ASD is because that's what I thought it was, as a seven year old. Now that I am eleven, I now understand that the word "disease" may not have been the "official" term to use. Please know that when I was diagnosed at 14 months, my parents were told that I would never speak. As you can see, those statements proved incorrect. Rather than complaining about my usage of the word disease, please rejoice in the fact that I am speaking. The point of the video was to show that even though I have autism, God has worked miracles in my life.

Sincerely, Patrick

Additional Thoughts on Autism

Want to learn more about autism? Here's a quick overview that includes helpful suggestions about how to support family members and friends who are on that difficult journey.

Understand

A quick overview of what autism is...and isn't:

- Autism is a developmental disorder, not mental illness.

- The Centers for Disease Control and Prevention reported data from a 2008 study indicated 1 in 88 children have some form of autism.

- The National Institute of Neurological Disorders and Stroke reports that males are four times more likely to have autism than females.

- The Autism Research Institute reports that diagnoses of autism have grown 600% in the last 10 years.

- Autism is now more common than Down syndrome.

- Autism varies widely in its severity and symptoms.

- Research has not yet identified conclusive "triggers" that cause autism in children.

The following behaviors are among those used to diagnose autism:

- Impaired ability to make friends with peers

- Inability to initiate or sustain a conversation with others

- Lack of imagination or play

- Repetitive or unusual use of language

- Preoccupation with certain objects or subjects

- Inflexible adherence to specific routines or rituals

Support

How you can support loved ones:

- Listen.

- Be patient.

- Extend grace and understanding.

- Welcome them into your community, neighborhood, home, and hearts.

- Ask questions…they are happy to share what they know.

- Remember that they are trying to live a normal life, just like you.

- Be available.

- Love them.

Connect

Recommended autism resources, websites, and organizations:

- *Autism's False Prophets: Bad Science, Risky Medicine and the Search for a Cure*, Paul A. Offit, M.D.

- *Disconnected Kids*, Dr. Robert Melillo.

- *Since We're Friends: An Autism Picture Book*, Celeste Shally & David Harrington.

- *Ten Things Every Child with Autism Wishes You Knew*, Ellen Notbohm.

- **Association for Science in Autism Treatment**
  asatonline.org

- **Autism National Committee**
  autcom.org

- **Autism Network International**
  ani.ac

- **Autism Research Institute**
  autism.com

- **Autism Society**
  autism-society.org

Personal Spiritual Growth

Connecting to the Topic

Molding Me

Reflect on the following questions, and jot down your thoughts in the space provided. (You won't have to share these answers aloud—this is just for you.)

- If you asked a friend to tell you what she thinks is shaping your life, what would your friend say are the things that are influencing you the most?

_____

_____

_____

_____

- What are things that you would like to have shaping your life that are not shaping it right now?

_____

_____

_____

_____

Taking Time

Discuss:

• What keeps you from spending time with God?

_____

_____

_____

Connecting With God

One mom can read these verses aloud to the table group:

Study this Book of Instruction continually. Meditate on it day and night so you will be sure to obey everything written in it. Only then will you prosper and succeed in all you do. (Joshua 1:8)

I lie awake thinking of you, meditating on you through the night. (Psalm 63:6)

Discuss:

• Studying God's Word continually or meditating on it "day and night" might not be logistically possible for most of us. But what are some simple ways you can encounter God's Word throughout the day? Share your thoughts, and jot down any you want to remember.

_____

_____

_____

Have one mom read these verses:

But Jesus often withdrew to the wilderness for prayer. (Luke 5:16)

One day soon afterward Jesus went up on a mountain to pray, and he prayed to God all night. (Luke 6:12)

Discuss:

- What do these verses tell you about the importance Jesus placed on talking with God? Explain. What can we learn from his example?

_____

_____

_____

- It may not be practical for us to withdraw from the responsibilities of family life to pray. But how can conversations with God be part of our daily lives?

_____

_____

_____

Connecting to My Life

- Ideas you have used, or would like to use, to create time with God:

_____

_____

_____

_____

_____

_____

_____

As you reflect, think about the importance of your relationship with God. Listen in silence to hear him calling you to spend time with him.

After listening, tear a piece of the foil from your mask, and shape it into something that reminds you of how important a friendship with God is to you. It might be the shape of a heart or a cross or anything that has meaning to you. Tape your piece of shaped foil in the spot available here.

Additional Thoughts on Personal Spiritual Growth

Spending time with God might be a new idea for you. Maybe you didn't go to church when you were younger or you went to a church that didn't encourage its people to spend time alone with God. But our hearts want to know God.

Consider what Psalm 42:1 says: "As the deer longs for streams of water, so I long for you, O God." Or Psalm 63:1, which says, "O God, you are my God; I earnestly search for you. My soul thirsts for you; my whole body longs for you in this parched and weary land where there is no water."

Can you hear the longing in the writer's voice? Can you see his hand over his heart as he says, "God, I am desperate for you. My heart and soul are thirsty, and only you can quench my longing." Are you like the writer of this psalm? Is your heart thirsty to know God better? Spend a few minutes writing a letter to God. Tell him about the thirst in your soul, and ask him to satisfy it like nothing else can.

_____

_____

_____

_____

_____

_____

_____

_____

_____

_____

It's a *Miracle!*

Connecting to the Topic

Katie Mahon Interview

Discuss the following questions with your group:

• What's your reaction to what you just saw?

_____

_____

_____

• Given that Ted Bundy confessed to murdering more than 30 women, why do you think Katie was spared and they weren't?

_____

_____

_____

• Why do you think some people experience miracles and others don't?

_____

_____

_____

The Miracle Chase

People fear miracles because they fear being changed.
Though ignoring them will change you also. —Leif Enger

Discuss:

• Do you agree with this quote? Why or why not?

_____

_____

Connecting With God

The Bible is *packed* with miracle stories—accounts like these…

‣ The sun standing still for an entire day. (Joshua 10:12-14)

‣ A woman turning into a pillar of salt. (Genesis 19:26)

‣ A donkey speaking. (Numbers 22:21-35)

‣ The sudden deaths of every firstborn son in Egypt.
  (Exodus 12:29)

‣ Jesus feeding 4,000 hungry people with just seven loaves of
  bread and a couple of fish. (Mark 8:1-8)

‣ Jesus telling a follower to go catch a fish, knowing that in the
  fish's mouth would be the exact amount of money needed to
  pay taxes. (Matthew 17:24-27)

‣ Jesus raising his friend Lazarus from the dead. (John 11:38-44)

‣ Jesus himself rising from the dead. (Matthew 28:1-10)

Discuss:

• What do you think the purpose of miracles might be?

_____

_____

_____

Connecting to My Life

Discuss:

- What are some things I can do to help me notice those moments in which God intersects with my life?

_____

_____

_____

_____

_____

_____

Additional Thoughts on Miracles

Take time to reflect on the following questions this week:

- How do you know if something unexplainable is a miracle, a coincidence, or something else?

_____

_____

_____

_____

- Why do some people experience miracles, while others don't?

_____

_____

_____

_____

- In John 5:6, Jesus asked a lame beggar "Would you like to get well?" before actually healing him. What role do our desires play in whether or not we experience miracles?

_____

_____

_____

_____

- What stands in your way of believing in God? What feeds your belief?

_____

_____

_____

_____

- If a miracle interrupted your life, would you be thankful? And which would you appreciate most—the miracle or Miracle Maker?

_____

_____

_____

_____

- How would experiencing a miracle change you?

_____

_____

_____

_____

Children and Spiritual Growth

Connecting to the Topic

Stop and Smell the Roses

In groups of three or four, brainstorm about five different ways you can see God in the everyday things around you and how you could use those things to teach your children about a specific characteristic of God.

Ways I Can See God Around Me   **Characteristic of God**

_____   _____

_____   _____

_____   _____

_____   _____

_____   _____

Connecting With God

One mom in the group can read these verses aloud.

Listen, O Israel! The Lord is our God, the Lord alone. And you must love the Lord your God with all your heart, all your soul, and all your strength. And you must commit yourselves wholeheartedly to these commands that I am giving you today.

Repeat them again and again to your children. Talk about them when you are at home and when you are on the road, when you are going to bed and when you are getting up. Tie them to your hands and wear them on your forehead as reminders. Write them on the doorposts of your house and on your gates. (Deuteronomy 6:4-9)

For he issued his laws to Jacob; he gave his instructions to Israel. He commanded our ancestors to teach them to their children, so the next generation might know them—even the children not yet born—and they in turn will teach their own children. So each generation should set its hope anew on God, not forgetting his glorious miracles and obeying his commands. Then they will not be like their ancestors— stubborn, rebellious, and unfaithful, refusing to give their hearts to God. (Psalm 78:5-8)

Discuss:

- What do these verses say are the benefits of teaching your kids about God? Are there others not mentioned in these verses?

  _____

  _____

- God instructed the Israelites to tie his commandments to their hands and foreheads. What do you think would have been the benefit of this? In what ways could we accomplish that same benefit today?

  _____

  _____

- How do these verses encourage you as you seek to teach your children spiritual truth?

  _____

  _____

Connecting to My Life

- Ways I can teach my kids about God that I've tried, thought about trying, or that someone else tried:

_____

_____

_____

_____

_____

_____

_____

Additional Thoughts on Children and Spiritual Growth

As you look for ways to help your children grow closer to God, keep these thoughts in mind:

- **See the sacred in the ordinary.** Attach "God thoughts" to daily activities. Bathing a child can remind you of baptism, and talking with one another can remind you of the gift of prayer.

- **Be alert to teachable moments.** Put up your "God antennae." For example, use the media as a teaching tool that sparks discussions.

- **Just "be" with your kids.** Simply be present without an agenda. When you stop trying so hard, it's freeing—and you'll actually relate better.

- **Realize your family doesn't have to be perfect.** Read the Bible together to see that God's grace was—and still is— sufficient for imperfect people.

Want more? Teaching your kids about God is a task you don't have to do alone. There are many books available as well as some websites that have fun, creative ideas aimed at helping parents teach their children about the Bible. Take a few minutes to check these out:

Online resources:

- Group at Home (group.com/at-home)

- Focus on the Family (focusonthefamily.com)

- CBH Ministries (cbhministries.org)

- Thriving Family Faith Archives (thrivingfamily.com)

Books:

- *13 Most Important Bible Lessons for Kids About God*, Group Publishing. This is written as a group study, but the lessons are easily adapted for families.

- *Mealtime Moments*, Focus on the Family.

- *Streams in the Desert for Kids*, L.B.E. Cowman.

- *Instant Family Devotions*, Mike Nappa and Jill Wuellner.

The Art of Listening

Connecting to the Topic

Listening Warm-Up

Draw the design your partner describes to you.

Listening Styles

People-oriented listeners
...**care deeply about others and their feelings.** You can sense their empathy, but they may become so caring they lose perspective.

Content-oriented listeners
...**zero in more on data than feelings.** Because they're seeking information, they may not listen carefully if the person speaking lacks credentials.

Action-oriented listeners
...**want to settle on action steps.** They're listening so they can get things done—and they do. But because they're pushing for action, they can become controlling.

Time-oriented listeners
...**care about the clock—a lot.** They're eager to have speakers get to the point so the conversation can wrap up and they can move on.

Discuss:

• Which of these listening styles is closest to yours?

_____

_____

Story Time

Use one of the following questions (or one of your own if you have one in mind) to start a conversation with your partner.

• How would you like to be remembered?

• What are you proudest of in your life?

• What are the most important lessons you've learned in life?

• What's your earliest memory?

• Who was the most important person in your life? Can you tell me about him or her?

• Who's had the biggest influence on your life? What lessons did that person teach you?

- Who's been the kindest to you in your life?

- Are there any words of wisdom you'd like to pass along to me?

- When in life have you felt most alone?

- How has your life been different than what you'd imagined?

- Do you have any regrets?

- What do you think your future holds?

- Is there something about me that you've always wanted to know but have never asked?

Connecting to My Life

- A person whose story is important to me is...

_____

- The question I would most like to ask them is...

_____

_____

Additional Thoughts on the Art of Listening

Take some time to reflect on the following thoughts this week.

For he has not ignored or belittled the suffering of the needy. He has not turned his back on them, but has listened to their cries for help. (Psalm 22:24)

In my desperation I prayed, and the Lord listened; he saved me from all my troubles. (Psalm 34:6)

Let the wise listen to these proverbs and become even wiser. Let those with understanding receive guidance. (Proverbs 1:5)

To one who listens, valid criticism is like a gold earring or other gold jewelry. (Proverbs 25:12)

Anyone with ears to hear should listen and understand! (Luke 14:35)

The goal of listening is to fully understand what's being said. Unfortunately, our own assumptions, beliefs, and judgments make that difficult—we tend to filter messages and miss their meaning. Use these six techniques to more actively engage in listening—and to become a better listener!

- **Be attentive.** The best listening happens when you're focused on the person speaking. Set aside other concerns during the conversation so you can give your complete attention. If possible, take your conversation somewhere that limits distractions.

- **Demonstrate that you're listening.** Use your body to signal that you're listening. Nod occasionally. Smile. Be sure your posture is open and inviting. Lean forward slightly. Now and then offer a small reassuring verbal comment like "yes" or "I see."

- **Make sure you understand.** Periodically check to see if your understanding of what was shared is accurate. Summarize what you heard, and give the speaker the opportunity to either correct you or expand on what you said. One way to do this is to say, "I think I hear you saying..." and then repeat what you think was said.

- **Listen...don't judge.** Allow the speaker to finish, without interrupting or challenging his or her facts, opinions, or version of the story. Be sure the speaker feels heard and has said all he or she wants to say.

- **Respond respectfully—especially if you're listening to someone who's upset with you.** By listening, you're gaining information and perspective and setting the tone for a civil conversation. Be aware that while the other person in your conversation may not listen well to you, you can still choose to be respectful. In your responses be open and honest, candid and kind. Treat the other person as you would like to be treated.

- **Make it a three-way conversation.** Invite God to become a partner in the conversation. A silent prayer asking for patience, kindness, and an understanding heart will make you a better listener. And when it comes to listening well, we need all the help we can get!

Exercise and *Health*
for Mom and Family

Connecting to the Topic

Read through this list of ideas for affordable exercise fun together. Take turns around the table reading each item.

- Throughout your family evening and weekend time together, take frequent 10-minute exercise breaks. (Homework will be more fun with jumping jacks involved!)

- Get each of your kids (and yourself!) a pedometer. They'll *love* seeing how far they walk each day!

- Park at the edge of the parking lot wherever you go, and model to your kids how to take advantage of small ways to incorporate exercise into your day.

- Plan a family dance party, and let each person play a few favorite songs while you each teach the family your "moves."

Now brainstorm some of your own ideas with your group. What ideas have you tried or thought of trying? Jot ideas you want to remember here.

_____

_____

_____

_____

_____

Connecting With God

One woman in each group can read this Scripture. Then discuss the questions that follow with your group.

Don't you realize that your body is the temple of the Holy Spirit, who lives in you and was given to you by God? You do not belong to yourself, for God bought you with a high price. So you must honor God with your body. (1 Corinthians 6:19-20)

Discuss:

• What do you think it means to honor God with your body?

_____

_____

_____

• How can these verses change the way you think about your body?

_____

_____

_____

• How can you model this for your children?

_____

_____

_____

Another woman in your group can read this verse aloud:

I discipline my body like an athlete, training it to do what it should. (1 Corinthians 9:27)

Discuss:

- What things get in the way of you disciplining your body?

_____

_____

_____

- How can exercise and a healthy lifestyle help you be more connected to God and his plan for your life?

_____

_____

_____

Connecting to My Life

My Fitness Formula

Write a one- to two-sentence summary of your commitment to lead your family in a more healthy and active lifestyle. It might sound something like this:

My fitness formula is to create a fun and healthy environment that helps my children to grow up valuing themselves because God made and loves them. I commit this plan to God and ask that he would lead me and my family to a healthier lifestyle so we can serve him.

This is just an example. Now, create your own fitness formula!

My fitness formula is...

_____

_____

_____

_____

Additional Thoughts on Exercise

Take time to reflect on this verse and the following questions in the week ahead.

All athletes are disciplined in their training. They do it to win a prize that will fade away, but we do it for an eternal prize. (1 Corinthians 9:25)

• What eternal prize are you training for?

_____

_____

_____

_____

_____

_____

• How can you help your kids train for that same prize?

_____

_____

_____

_____

_____

_____

Take time to pray this week that God will be your family's ultimate personal trainer!

Try one of these fun and affordable exercise ideas this week.

- Take play dates to a new level—actually *play* with your kids! Tennis, swimming, dodge ball, even playing catch in the front yard—they *all* count as exercise and fun.

- Have weekly pedometer contests to see who can walk the farthest and who can increase their numbers by the most.

- Forget the elevator!

- Replace all table chairs in the house with fitness balls.

- Be spontaneous! Hop up and do push-ups or run in place during commercials.

- Create an obstacle course in your backyard. Jump over baskets, run around cones, carry buckets of water, and toss a ball at a target.

- Time your activities. See who can run around the block the fastest, who can finish a set of sit-ups the quickest, or see how many push-ups each person can do in 1 minute.

- Set up exercise stations in the basement, and have family members rotate through the circuit. A jump rope at one station, dumbbells (or books) at another, jumping jacks at another—it doesn't have to cost a lot to exercise together!

- As a family, work toward participating in a healthy event together—a hike in a new location or a 5K race will give you all a common exercise goal.

- Schedule walk-and-talk dates with each of your kids.

- Use exercise as a reward. Good grades? Hooray! Now you can take those tennis lessons!

- Be the influence. Find something active you love to do, and your kids will catch your commitment and enthusiasm.

Notes

_____

_____

_____

_____

_____

_____

_____

_____

_____

_____

_____

_____

_____

_____

_____

_____

How to *Live* Before You *Die:*
Embracing life to the fullest

Connecting to the Topic

Five Characteristics of People Who Feel Fulfilled:

- Gratitude

- Curiosity

- An ability to love and be loved

- Zest for life

- Spirituality

Wisdom From Dr. Sasha Vukelja

In your group, take turns reading the following quotes. Then, have each woman share which quote most resonates with her and why.

- "You have a terminal illness called life."

- "It wasn't recovery anymore; it was discovery."

- "Ask the unexpected question."

- "When someone is dying, you don't have to say goodbye. You can just say, 'I'll see you.'"

- "You can do so much more than you think you can do, because God built us like that."

Connecting With God

Wisdom From Jesus

In your group, take turns reading the following quotes (from The Message version of the Bible). Then have each woman share which quote most resonates with her and why.

- "First things first. Your business is life, not death. Follow me. Pursue life." —Jesus (Matthew 8:22)

- "Give away your life; you'll find life given back, but not merely given back—given back with bonus and blessing. Giving, not getting, is the way. Generosity begets generosity." —Jesus (Luke 6:38)

- "If you grasp and cling to life on your terms, you'll lose it, but if you let that life go, you'll get life on God's terms." —Jesus (Luke 17:33)

Connecting to My Life

- What helps you live a full and satisfying life?

_____

_____

_____

_____

_____

_____

_____

_____

Additional Thoughts on Living Life to the Fullest

When you have a few moments to yourself, read this devotion and reflect.

Whatever you do, do well. (Ecclesiastes 9:10)

"Live in the moment." How often have we heard that? It's supposed to be a stress buster and good for our health. But what does it really mean? We text at meals, converse on phones while shopping, and some people play games during sermons! It seems we're so busy with our daily lives, one moment blurs into the next.

Thinking about this, I came to the conclusion that the word *live* is the clue. *Live* in this sense does not simply mean breathe the air, keep the body in full faculty, and sustain your being. It's far more expansive. In my way of thinking, it means to take the present and celebrate it, eat it up, let it flow in you like a rhythmic dance, a lovely scent to breathe in.

"Fine," you say, "that's very nice, but at this moment I'm changing the baby's diapers. Hardly a celebration, and I'm desperately trying *not* to breathe in."

I know. I've been there. But nonetheless, it is a moment of life.

Often we're so busy thinking about what we need to get done this evening or what awkward situation happened at work yesterday that we fail to grasp what is happening now. Now is what we have, and not by accident. People, events, even tasks enter our daily lives, and repeatedly we give them very little heed, when indeed they are a respected part of God's design for us. He, by his gracious Spirit, is present with his children. Therefore, nothing is insignificant. Whether in the midst of a mundane situation or a life-changing event, it is ours and belongs to no one else. Embrace it.

Whatever place you are in—preparing for the Boston Marathon or sidelined by illness, raising a family or on your own, washing dishes or signing a multi-million dollar contract, and yes, even changing your baby's diapers—this is your moment. See Jesus in it, and live fully.

- What is the most "insignificant" thing you do each day? Ask God to show you how to make that meaningful…and to appreciate that task in a new way!

_____

_____

_____

_____

_____

_____

_____

_____

_____

_____

_____

_____

_____

_____

_____

Friendships

Connecting Together

No man is an island,
Entire of itself,
Every man is a piece of the continent,
A part of the main. —John Donne

Connecting With God

One mom in the group can read these verses aloud:

A friend is always loyal, and a brother is born to help in time of need. (Proverbs 17:17)

There are "friends" who destroy each other, but a real friend sticks closer than a brother. (Proverbs 18:24)

The heartfelt counsel of a friend is as sweet as perfume and incense. (Proverbs 27:9)

As iron sharpens iron, so a friend sharpens a friend. (Proverbs 27:17)

Discuss:

• Tell about a friend who represents one of these verses to you.

_____

_____

- Which of these verses do you find most difficult to live out as a friend? Why?

_____

_____

_____

Have another mom read these verses aloud:

> When three of Job's friends heard of the tragedy he had suffered, they got together and traveled from their homes to comfort and console him. (Job 2:11)

> Some men came carrying a paralyzed man on a sleeping mat. They tried to take him inside to Jesus, but they couldn't reach him because of the crowd. So they went up to the roof and took off some tiles. Then they lowered the sick man on his mat down into the crowd, right in front of Jesus. Seeing their faith, Jesus said to the man, "Young man, your sins are forgiven." (Luke 5:18-20)

Discuss:

- Tell about a time you were sick or in need and a friend came to help you. What did it do to your friendship?

_____

_____

_____

- Luke 5:20 says that Jesus told the young man his sins were forgiven after seeing the faith of his friends. How does _your_ faith affect your friendships?

_____

_____

_____

Connecting to My Life

A Friendship Garden

- Things I can do to nurture strong friendships…

_____

_____

_____

_____

_____

_____

_____

_____

_____

_____

_____

_____

_____

_____

_____

_____

_____

_____

Additional Thoughts on Friendships

A good friendship is like a sweet aroma. It's soothing to the soul and nourishing to the heart. We are all drawn to find other women who are comfortable and comforting. But what about those who are a bit rough around the edges? The woman who's a bit socially awkward or has a coarse personality. The woman who doesn't have many friends. You know who she is. Her heart yearns for connection and friendship, but it's difficult to see past the outer layer of discomfort.

Are you willing to take on a challenge this week? Try reaching out to someone who might be an uncomfortable fit. Take a few minutes and talk to God about it. He can open your eyes and heart to someone new—to someone who takes a bit more work than you're used to. Then ask her to join you and a few friends for lunch. Maybe she could meet you at the park for a kids' play date or just to enjoy the fresh air. Whatever you choose to do, rest assured that your friendship will be a sweet aroma and nourishment to her soul. God will smile, and your heart will be blessed.

Fighting Fair:

A practical path to healthy conflict

Connecting to the Topic

What's Your Fight Type?

Read the following descriptions of the four fight types, and discuss the questions that follow.

Competitive fighters

...like to win. They're often blunt, direct, and quick to express their viewpoints. They like to be acknowledged as right and may fail to empathize with others in the disagreement.

Collaborative fighters

...are team players. They're good listeners and are often expressive and flexible. The downside: To avoid tough issues, they might sidestep conflict or not be clear about what they want.

Conciliatory fighters

...are peacemakers. They're often quiet and serene, but because they avoid conflict if at all possible, they tend to not own their thoughts and will too quickly accept solutions offered by others.

Cautious fighters

...need time and information to fight. They focus on facts, ask questions to clarify others' positions, and then build a case for their viewpoint. They operate like attorneys going to court.

Discuss:

- What's your fight type?

_____

_____

- Why do you think that's you? Give an example.

_____

_____

Qualities of a Good Fight

A good fight—one that's healthy and brings combatants closer together—includes these four CORE essentials.*

Cooperation—When everyone involved wants resolution and is willing to work together to find an answer, a win-win solution is possible. But when someone won't cooperate, fights tend to drag on...and on.

Ownership—Blaming others for the conflict turns us into victims. Better: Have the courage to take responsibility for your feelings and admit openly what you've done to contribute to the disagreement.

Respect—Respect builds safety within relationships, letting everyone risk being open and truthful. Belittling comments, eye-rolling, and sarcasm shut down communication...and solutions.

Empathy—Research indicates 90 percent of marital spats can be resolved if couples will see issues from each other's perspective. Seek to understand the feelings and motivations of those with whom you're fighting.

*Information from Drs. Les and Leslie Parrott, _The Good Fight: How Conflict Can Bring You Closer._ (Worthy Publishing)

Characteristics of Dirty Fighters

Dirty fighters...

- **drag in past mistakes or other issues.** They muddy the water by tossing in everything they're mad about at one time, shifting between issues.

- **assume they know others' thoughts and motivations.** They attack based on what they think is meant, not what's been said. They don't ask what others think and feel—and then listen.

- **use absolutes.** Is it true she *never* listens? He *always* exaggerates? Though absolutes are seldom accurate and often put people on the defensive, dirty fighters use them.

- **shout—or use rude language.** Volume and tone matter, as do words used. Dirty fighters indulge in name calling, swearing, and rants.

- **let body language scream.** They roll their eyes. Smirk. Sigh as they check their watches. They signal disrespect and use sarcasm.

- **fight when they (or others) are tired.** Or hungry. Or overly angry. Or pressured for time. Dirty fighters don't consider whether others are ready to fight.

- **debate details.** Dirty fighters focus on the details of a perceived transgression rather than the larger picture of why they're upset.

- **walk away without saying when they'll be back.** Taking a cool-down period can be helpful, but dirty fighters stalk off without negotiating a time when they'll be back to finish the fight.

- **win at all costs.** Winning the argument seems to matter more than preserving the relationship.

Characteristics of Fair Fighters

Fair fighters...

- **take responsibility.** They own their contribution to the conflict, using "I" statements rather than only talking about what others have done. "You" is a word that points fingers; using the word "I" shows ownership.

- **are honest about their thoughts and feelings.** They're kind—but clear. They don't expect others to read their minds or accurately guess their feelings.

- **listen.** *Really* listen. They summarize what they've heard to be sure they've got it right—and so others know they've been heard. They make sure everyone involved has time to share points of view.

- **discuss problems, not people.** They focus on the problem to be solved, not what's wrong with the people involved.

- **deal with conflict promptly.** They don't let small things become bigger with time.

- **set a time limit.** If they can't settle an issue in 30 minutes, they work to schedule a time for round two.

- **tackle conflict as a team.** They work to get a clear definition of what the problem is—and don't move forward until there's agreement on that point and a willingness of all involved to move toward a solution.

- **think "win-win."** They look for solutions, not someone to blame. They compromise where they can and give a little to get a little.

- **invite God to help**—both to reach a solution and for relationships to be strengthened.

Connecting With God

Words kill, words give life; they're either poison or fruit—you choose. (Proverbs 18:21, The Message)

Additional Thoughts on Fighting Fair

Take time to reflect on one of the following thoughts this week.

• As you go about your week, think about the techniques you learned for fighting fair. Who might you practice them with?

_____

_____

_____

_____

• A summary of Les and Leslie Parrott's insights is that learning to fight fair is worth the effort. Fair fights are good fights—they let us be ourselves and speak the truth as we see it, clear the air, shed light on situations, and make relationships stronger. Choose one of those four benefits to fighting fair to work on this week.

_____

_____

_____

_____

• James 4:1 says, "What is causing the quarrels and fights among you? Don't they come from the evil desires at war within you?" How might the behaviors of dirty fighters reflect the evil desires James talks about? How could the behaviors of fair fighters help counteract those evil desires?

_____

_____

_____

_____

Notes

Teen Adventures

Connecting to the Topic

Share the answer to the following question with your group:

• What word or phrase best describes your teen years?

_____

_____

_____

With your group, brainstorm answers to the following questions:

• What negative qualities do you associate with teens today?

_____

_____

_____

• What positive qualities do you associate with teens today?

_____

_____

_____

Connecting With God

One woman can read these verses aloud to the group.

Dear brothers and sisters, when I was with you I couldn't talk to you as I would to spiritual people. I had to talk as though you belonged to this world or as though you were infants in the Christian life. I had to feed you with milk, not with solid food, because you weren't ready for anything stronger. And you still aren't ready, for you are still controlled by your sinful nature. You are jealous of one another and quarrel with each other. Doesn't that prove you are controlled by your sinful nature? Aren't you living like people of the world? (1 Corinthians 3:1-3)

There is much more we would like to say about this, but it is difficult to explain, especially since you are spiritually dull and don't seem to listen. You have been believers so long now that you ought to be teaching others. Instead, you need someone to teach you again the basic things about God's word. You are like babies who need milk and cannot eat solid food. For someone who lives on milk is still an infant and doesn't know how to do what is right. Solid food is for those who are mature, who through training have the skill to recognize the difference between right and wrong. (Hebrews 5:11-14)

I am telling you these things now while I am still with you. But when the Father sends the Advocate as my representative— that is, the Holy Spirit—he will teach you everything and will remind you of everything I have told you. I am leaving you with a gift—peace of mind and heart. And the peace I give is a gift the world cannot give. So don't be troubled or afraid. (John 14:25-27)

Discuss:

- What part have the experiences from your teen years played in your growth as a woman?

- How do your assumptions about the teen years affect the way you interact with teens today?

- How could insights from these verses be applied in the way you parent your teen—or come alongside a friend who is parenting a teen?

Connecting to My Life

The Soap Experience

Discuss:

• How is parenting a teen like trying to hold a bar of wet soap?

_____

_____

• In what ways can you avoid holding on to a teen too tightly?

_____

_____

• In what ways can you avoid holding on to a teen too loosely?

_____

_____

God is telling me...

A Challenge for This Week

Every time you wash your hands this week, pray for wisdom in parenting your child—no matter that child's age—that you would know the right way to balance holding on to them too tightly and holding them too loosely.

Did you wash your hands today?

Name and Contact Information:

_____

_____

_____

_____

_____

_____

_____

_____

_____

_____

_____

_____

_____

_____

Additional Thoughts on Teen Adventures

Take time to reflect on the following verse and parenting insights this week:

> So let's not get tired of doing what is good. At just the right time we will reap a harvest of blessing if we don't give up. Therefore, whenever we have the opportunity, we should do good to everyone—especially to those in the family of faith. (Galatians 6:9-10)

- Love your teenager. Love includes affirmation and appropriate discipline.

- Show honor and respect to your teenager. You have to earn their trust, just as they have to earn yours.

- Have fun with your teenager. Don't be serious all the time, and take advantage of the "little" moments when you can.

- Set rules, but keep them simple. Unreasonable expectations will always bring about undesirable results.

- Live a godly example. Admit your faults, and commit to personal spiritual growth.

- Seek and foster supportive relationships. Life, including parenting, isn't meant to be done in isolation.

- Don't be too hard on yourself. Tearing yourself down as a parent will undermine your effectiveness as a parent.

- Enjoy the journey. Remember that each moment—good and bad—is a memory to build on and a step forward in the adventure of parenting your teen.

Notes

_____

_____

_____

_____

_____

_____

_____

_____

_____

_____

_____

_____

_____

_____

_____

_____

_____

_____

Follow Your Dreams

Connecting to the Topic

Keys to Following Your Dreams

Following dreams and achieving success means...

- **making sure the dream you're following is *your* dream.** It's hard to follow someone else's dream for your life. You can't sustain enthusiasm.

- **investing time and effort.** Following dreams often requires us to learn new things, develop new skills.

- **focusing...yet staying flexible.** People who follow their dreams aren't derailed by challenges. But they *are* realistic. Learn to improvise. Focus on what you *can* do, not on what you *can't* do.

Connecting With God

Seek the Kingdom of God above all else, and live righteously, and he will give you everything you need. —Jesus
(Matthew 6:33)

Additional Thoughts on Following Your Dreams

Take time this week to reflect on the following Bible verses. How can these thoughts encourage you as you follow your dreams?

Take delight in the Lord, and he will give you your heart's desires. (Psalm 37:4)

"For I know the plans I have for you," says the Lord. "They are plans for good and not for disaster, to give you a future and a hope." (Jeremiah 29:11)

Yet I still dare to hope when I remember this: The faithful love of the Lord never ends! His mercies never cease. Great is his faithfulness; his mercies begin afresh each morning. (Lamentations 3:21-23)

For we are God's masterpiece. He has created us anew in Christ Jesus, so we can do the good things he planned for us long ago. (Ephesians 2:10)

Faith is the confidence that what we hope for will actually happen; it gives us assurance about things we cannot see. (Hebrews 11:1)

Planning Nutritious Meals

Connecting to the Topic

A Nutritious Adventure

Read through this list of ideas for making good nutrition a part of your family's meal plan. Take turns in your group reading each item.

- Let kids read the weekly grocery store circulars, either paper or online. Let them identify what they think are healthy choices, and then discuss the nutritional value of their choices.

- Have kids clip grocery coupons for the healthy items you've chosen.

- Make a meal chart, and let kids pick a healthy food from each category: protein, veggie, and starch.

- Have several theme nights this month—Italian, Greek, or Mexican—and let your kids look up healthy recipes to try.

Now brainstorm some of your own ideas with your group. Write the ones you want to remember here:

_____

_____

_____

_____

Connecting With God

One woman can read this verse aloud to the group. Then discuss the questions that follow.

So whether you eat or drink, or whatever you do, do it all for the glory of God. (1 Corinthians 10:31)

• What do you think it means to give glory to God by eating and drinking?

_____

_____

_____

• How can giving glory to God help us make better choices when it comes to food and nutrition?

_____

_____

_____

Nutrition Wisdom

One woman can read this verse aloud to the group. Then discuss the question that follows.

Do you like honey? Don't eat too much, or it will make you sick! (Proverbs 25:16)

• What nutritional guidelines could you draw out of this verse—beyond just thinking about honey?

_____

_____

_____

Connecting to My Life

Recipe for Success

Write a brief "Recipe for Success" that contains three steps you'll take—three "ingredients"—to create more nutritious meals for your family. Here's a sample:

1. Letting each of my kids choose which healthy foods we'll eat at a meal this week.

2. Reading ingredients and not buying anything my child can't pronounce or identify.

3. Committing to helping my family give glory to God in all they do, including the food choices they make.

This is just an example. Now create your own "Recipe for Success"!

My recipe for success to create more nutritious meals for my family includes these three ingredients...

1 _____

2 _____

3 _____

Additional Thoughts on Planning Nutritious Meals

Choose one of these ideas this week for making good nutrition a part of your family's meal plan. Circle the first one you'll try— and after you try it, write a note to keep track of how that went. Then choose another to try.

- Let kids keep track of the coupon savings, and if possible, put those savings toward a vacation or fun monthly outing.

- Have older kids help do the grocery shopping, buying only food with ingredients they can pronounce or identify.

- Let younger kids play "restaurant" as they offer various menu items—your fun responses can go a long way in teaching nutritious choices!

- Let each child choose a meal of the week, and have them help in the preparation.

- Commit to not eating anything that has a commercial—this will be a real eye-opener!

- Plan a picnic (even if it's in the living room) instead of eating out.

- Have a dipping dinner! Set out healthy dips and a variety of cheeses and vegetables as a meatless alternative.

- Have healthy snacks always available for grazing—a basket of healthy granola bars in the pantry or a drawer of cut-up veggies and fruit in the refrigerator. Kids will love the freedom of choice!

- Do a media detox—no TV for a set length of time—and see how it alters your eating habits and choices.

- Kids learn from you, so model healthy habits. Say, "I love eating broccoli because it has calcium that makes my bones strong."

- Assign kids jobs that go with each meal—getting the forks or filling water glasses, for example. The more you involve them in the process of family mealtime, the more you can casually talk to them about nutrition and health.

- Print an "in season" list of fruits and vegetables, and let kids choose their favorites to buy.

Be hungry for God! Carve out time to spend alone with him this week. Sit down with a favorite snack and cup of tea, and take time to read your Bible, pray, or just quietly enjoy your food and drink as you thank him for your family and the wonderful bounty he's provided for them.

Secrets of
Finding Contentment:
Living a satisfying life

Connecting Together

My Level of Contentment

Not contented at all   Very contented

Connecting to the Topic

Contentment Keys

Five keys that unlock contentment are…

1. **Love people, not possessions.** Having close, loving relationships helps us feel safe and supported. They give us a sense of wellbeing and community that possessions simply can't provide.

2. **Don't compare yourself with others.** When we compare ourselves to others, we pick people who have more of what we want. And that isn't a habit that leads to contentment.

3. **Appreciate what you have.** It's a matter of *choice*. Be happy with what you have, not what you don't.

4. **Choose friends and form relationships wisely.** There are people who build you up and those that tear you down. Encouragers and discouragers. You may be stuck with some discouragers, but what are you doing to even that out with a supply of encouragers too?

5. **Feed your spiritual life.** Having a purpose in life and a perspective when things go wrong both help you weather life's storms. And contentment rises with a personal relationship with God.

• The one or two keys to contentment that are a challenge for me:

_____

_____

_____

_____

_____

_____

• The one or two keys to contentment that come easily for me:

_____

_____

_____

_____

_____

_____

Connecting With God

Give away your life; you'll find life given back, but not merely given back—given back with bonus and blessing. Giving, not getting, is the way.—Jesus (Luke 6:38, The Message)

Connecting to My Life

- How can you use a key to contentment that comes easily to you to renew your sense of contentment this week?

_____

_____

_____

_____

_____

_____

- How can you work into your life a key to contentment that is a challenge to you and grow in your sense of contentment this week?

_____

_____

_____

_____

_____

_____

Additional Thoughts on Finding Contentment

The next time you need a little perspective on contentment, read this devotion.

Consider it pure joy, my brothers, whenever you face trials of many kinds. (James 1:2, NIV)

Reread the verse above. Can you believe it? James tells us to find joy in trials. Obviously, James didn't have a power-crazed boss or an amazingly loud and rude neighbor or a teenager who refused to wear anything but black. If he did, he'd certainly never have written this passage. Or...would he?

James knew a simple truth we need to accept: There's no escape from trials. He's not talking about the jury-duty kind of trials, but the ones that send us screaming for a therapist. To make matters worse, his suggestion is actually more of a command: When the crisis comes, consider it joy.

You may be one who thinks it would be easier to lose four dress sizes than to find joy in tough times. It seems impossible! Yet the Bible directs us to find joy. How? One trial at a time. Perhaps if we start to practice finding joy in the little trials, it may be easier to do when the bigger trials hit.

What if you've planned a camping trip—and it rains every day? Could you find joy in the damp tents and soggy sleeping bags? It will, after all, make for some great laughs in the future!

Or that long line at the grocery store—when you've still got fifteen other stops to make on your lunch break—is there joy to be found there? A song to hum, a smile to share with someone nearby, a moment to take a relaxing breath?

Finding joy in moments like these can help us be ready for the bigger trials. Sickness, financial woes, difficult relationships. Believe it or not, God can even help us find joy in these times of trial.

We need to determine in our hearts and heads to find some bit of joy in lesser trials such as banks lines, traffic lights, and whiny children. Once we've mastered this in the small things, joy will be easier to grasp in the larger ones. Practice makes perfect! God provides various journeys in each of our lives; some will not be joyful—yet there is joy on every path, if we learn to look for it!

Take a moment and list the trials, big or small, you've faced in the past two weeks. How could you have looked for joy? Keep the list handy. When another trial comes your way, look at your list again. Choose a joyful response.

_____

_____

_____

_____

_____

_____

_____

_____

_____

_____

_____

_____

_____

_____

_____

Notes

_____

_____

_____

_____

_____

_____

_____

_____

_____

_____

_____

_____

_____

_____

_____

_____

_____

Notes

Notes

_____

_____

_____

_____

_____

_____

_____

_____

_____

_____

_____

_____

_____

_____

_____

_____

_____